Walt Disney's
MICKEY AND FRIENDS

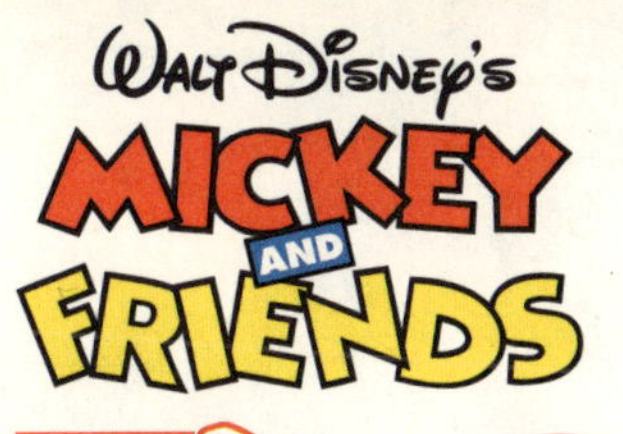

LET'S GO to the Vet

By Zoe Lewis
Illustrated by DiCicco Digital Arts

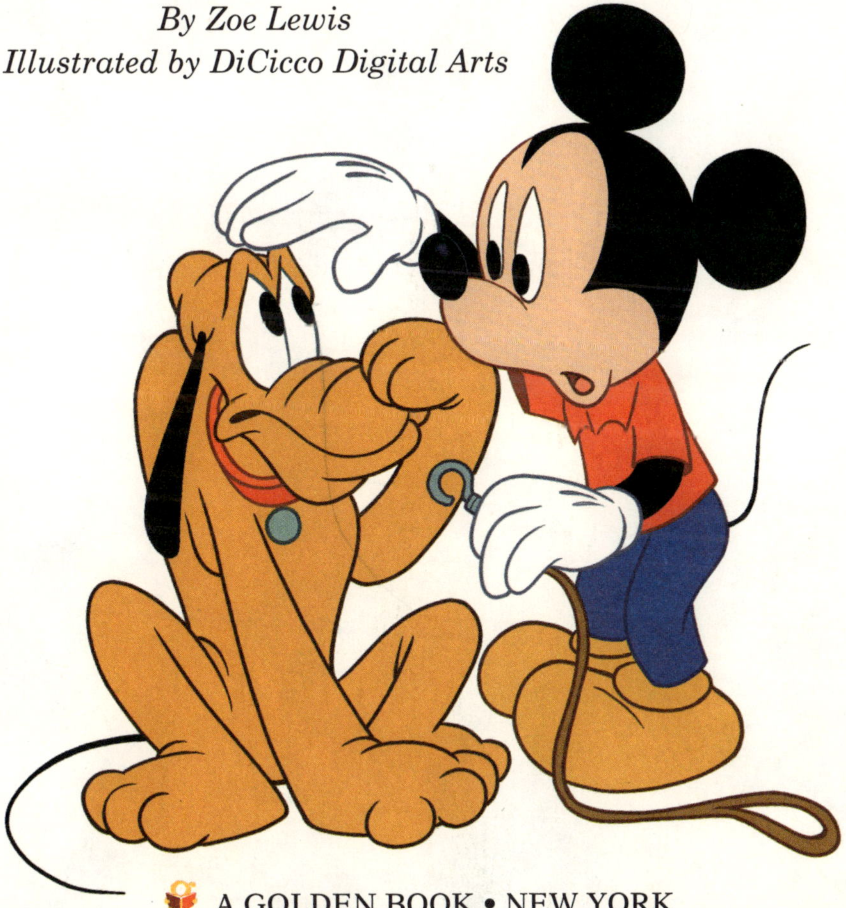

A GOLDEN BOOK • NEW YORK
Golden Books Publishing Company, Inc., Racine, Wisconsin 53404

 Library of Congress Catalog Card Number: 97-70001
ISBN: 0-307-98804-X
A MCMXCVII First Edition 1997

Mickey Mouse was opening his mail at home one day when Minnie burst in the door. She was waving a photograph of her beloved cat, Fluffy.

"She won!" Minnie cried. "Fluffy won second prize in the photo contest in *Pet Food Digest* magazine. Isn't that swell?"

"It sure is," said Mickey with a grin. "But here's something else that's swell. I entered Pluto in the contest, too—and he won *first* prize!"

Several days later, photographers showed up at Mickey's house with lots of equipment. Mickey explained to Pluto that it was time to pose for some pictures. The magazine wanted a photo story about the winner of the contest.

Minnie brought Fluffy to the photo shoot. Minnie didn't realize that Fluffy and Pluto were jealous of each other. When Pluto went over to sniff the cameras, Fluffy ran past and knocked things over. Everybody thought it was Pluto's fault.

"Watch where you're going, Pluto!" Mickey warned.

Finally, the cameras were ready.

"Pluto, look over here!" Mickey called for the third time. But Pluto couldn't keep his eyes on the camera. Fluffy had found his favorite toy and was playing with it. Pluto could see her out of the corner of his eye.

"Pluto, stop!" Mickey shouted, but it was no use.

Pluto couldn't stand it another minute. He had to get his toy back. He rushed at Fluffy, but the cat held onto the toy and growled. Pluto growled right back. Suddenly Fluffy reached out and swiped the dog across the nose with her claws.

"Fluffy! No, no!" said Minnie, scolding her cat.

Pluto was in pain. He wouldn't let Mickey look at the scratch on his nose. Mickey reached for Pluto's leash. "I'd better take you to the vet," he said. "We don't want to take any chances."

“Great!” said one of the photographers. “A veterinarian’s office is a good place to take some pictures.”

Mickey agreed that the camera crew could come along.

Soon they all arrived at Dr. Daisy Duck's office. Daisy had just finished with another patient. She told Mickey to bring Pluto into the examining room.

"Just let me wash my hands," she said. "Then I'll take a look at that scratch."

The photographers followed Pluto into the examining room. At first Daisy tried to shoo them away, but Mickey talked her into letting them stay.

“I feel terrible about this,” said Minnie as Daisy checked Pluto.

“Will he be okay, Doc?” Mickey asked.

Daisy nodded. “He’ll be fine. It’s not serious. I’m just going to put something on the scratch so it won’t get infected.”

"Is that it?" asked a photographer, when Daisy had finished.

"Aren't you going to operate?" said the other.

Daisy smiled. "There's no need for that," she said. "But I could give Pluto his yearly checkup. He's about due for one, anyway."

Mickey agreed to a checkup for Pluto.

"First I'll look at your fur, Pluto," said Daisy. "Good news—you're flea-free!"

Next she checked Pluto's eyes.

"Hold still," Daisy told the dog.

Daisy looked into Pluto's ears. "I think you had a bath this morning," she said. "Your ears are spotless."

Then Daisy looked at Pluto's mouth. "But I need to clean those teeth," she said.

Dr. Daisy used a stethoscope to listen to Pluto's heart. "A good, strong heartbeat," said Daisy.

Then Daisy asked Pluto to hop on the scale. "Fine! Your weight is just right," she announced.

"Now I'm going to clip your claws," Daisy told Pluto. "They're too long. But, don't worry, it won't hurt."

When the nail clipping was done, Daisy pulled out a large needle. “All I have left to do is give Pluto a shot,” she said. “Something to keep him healthy.”

Pluto whimpered and tried to hide. It seemed as if he didn’t like the idea of a shot. The photographers glanced at one another.

"It's not good if the contest winner looks scared," one muttered.

"Maybe we have another pet who can stand in for him," said another crew person. "Who came in second?"

Mickey took out some dog biscuits. He had brought them along just in case. When Pluto smelled something good, he sat up straight. Daisy gave him his shot, but Pluto didn't even blink. He just waited for Mickey to give him a snack.

"What a good dog!" Minnie exclaimed. Then she looked down at her cat. "By the way, Fluffy, it's almost time for your next checkup, too. We'll make a date with the doctor now."

Several weeks later, Minnie and Fluffy sat in the vet's waiting room, looking at Pluto's pictures in *Pet Food Digest* magazine.

"Doesn't he look handsome, Fluffy?" Minnie said. "When you get your shot today, I hope you'll behave as well as Pluto did. The doctor should be ready for you any second now. . . ."